How To Get What You Want

All you need to know on how to be a good Negotiator

Katherina C. Norton

Table of contents

Chapter 1

What Is a Negotiation?

The word "negotiation" describes a planned conversation that finds a mutually agreeable solution to a problem. Each side in a negotiation seeks to convince the other to accept their point of view. Given that there is some give and take during negotiations, one side will always prevail. But even a little concession must be made by the other.

All parties concerned attempt to prevent conflict via negotiation while agreeing on a compromise. Buyers and sellers, an employer and a potential employee, a government of two or more nations, or other parties may all be negotiating parties.
The Process of Negotiation
In negotiations, two or more parties work together to find a compromise or a solution that is acceptable to all parties to achieve a

certain end objective. One side will express its stance, and the other will either accept the terms or respond with a different one. Up until a settlement is reached by both sides, the procedure continues.

Before a negotiation starts, participants try to understand as much as they can about the other party's position, including its advantages and disadvantages, how to be ready to defend their views, and any potential counterarguments.

Negotiations may be a short period or a long period, depending on the situation. The duration of the negotiation might range from a few minutes to many hours in more complicated situations. For instance, a buyer and seller may haggle over the purchase of a vehicle for a few minutes or many hours. However, it can take months or even years for the governments of two or more nations to agree on the parameters of a trade agreement.

Where the Negotiations Happen

Many individuals believe that pricing and offerings are unchangeable and irrevocable. But that's not always the case. In actuality, many are adaptable. Agreements may be reached via negotiation in several different contexts. Several instances include:

lowering debt
reducing a home's asking price for sale
enhancing the terms of a contract
Getting a vehicle at a better price
Consider purchasing a brand-new SUV. The manufacturer's recommended retail price is often the starting point of the discussion between you and the salesperson (MSRP). The manufacturer advises the dealership to sell the automobile for this amount. Many people are unaware that, unless the brand or model is very popular, most dealerships normally sell below the MSRP. You may approach the dealer with a lower offer than the MSRP; the dealership may accept it or reject it. You may be able to drive away with a fantastic bargain even lower than the

vehicle's invoice price if you are skilled at haggling. This is the real cost to the dealer that the manufacturer imposes.

The ability to negotiate is crucial when taking a new job. The employee may negotiate other conditions, such as a greater salary, longer vacation time, better retirement benefits, and so forth. The employer's first offer of remuneration is often not the company's best offer. Because all future pay raises will be dependent on the first offer, negotiating a job offer is very crucial.

Important Negotiation Elements
Some various crucial components or criteria must be taken into consideration during negotiations if you want to succeed:

Who are the parties involved in the negotiation and what are their interests? What are everyone's backgrounds, and how does it influence where they stand in the conversation?

Relationships: How do the parties and their representatives in the negotiation get along? What impact does the parties' relationship have on the conditions of the negotiating process?

To achieve the parties' agreements via negotiation, how will the demands of the parties be effectively communicated? What is the best technique to communicate the demands and intended results? What guarantees do the parties have that their voices are being heard?

Alternatives: Are there any choices except what each party desires at the outset? Will the parties need to seek other resolutions if a straight agreement is not feasible?

Realistic Alternatives: Which alternatives could be effective in achieving a goal? Have the parties stated any areas where their expectations could be flexible?

Legitimate Claims: Are the demands and assurances made by each side true? What supporting facts do the parties provide to support their assertions and demonstrate the legitimacy of their demands? How will they ensure that the outcomes of the negotiations will be carried out?

Level of Commitment: How much dedication will it take to carry out the agreement reached during the negotiations? What is at risk for each party, and are efforts needed to accomplish the agreed-upon outcomes taken into account during negotiations?

The Steps in the Negotiating Process

Our daily lives involve a great deal of negotiation. Even when we don't realize it, we often engage in negotiation. Negotiating with your adolescent over a curfew might be as straightforward as discussing your income. No matter what you're negotiating or with whom, there are often several processes involved. The essential processes that most discussions need from beginning to completion have been underlined.

Prepare

There is a lot of preliminary work involved in the initial step. Being unprepared won't do you any good. Often, this begins with establishing and building the groundwork. What are your expectations? This is one important issue that you should be careful to address.

What do you want to achieve?

What kind of concession are you ready to make?

What happens if you don't accomplish your ultimate objective?

Decide on your negotiation approach and the tactics you'll use. Are you going to compete, be accommodating, or work together? This plan will need to be modified based on your desired results and ultimate goals. The next step is research. As much as you can, learn more about the other party.

If you're meeting your boss, for instance, be ready to explain why you deserve a raise. Your position may be strengthened by specific instances of your successes supported by concrete data and outcomes, recommendations from customers or colleagues, and any intentions you may have for professional advancement.

Transact Information

It's time to sit down with the other side, who has likely done their due diligence before sitting at the table, now that you've established the framework for your discussions. Both parties may now spell out the arguments they will use to support their positions to achieve their desired outcomes.

Here, communication is crucial. The ability to communicate clearly and fully is essential to the negotiating process. So don't cut corners when it comes to the specifics. Fewer details will need to be worked out in the future if you play your cards straight.

Therefore, while negotiating a contract, be as specific as you can about what you want to contribute, your terms, and what you hope to achieve. This may be accomplished orally, in writing, or via a presentation.

Clarify

You've both now expressed your stances and where you stand. Both you and the other person should be clear on what the other is seeking and what you are seeking. You want to make sure that you and the other person are on the same page, so this step is crucial.

Now is the opportunity to inquire if any kinks need to be worked out, if you need any further details, or if you have any queries that require clarification. Additionally, make sure the other side accepts your stance.

Bargain

It's time to start haggling now that all the information has been shared and both of you have clarity. The actual bargaining starts here. Additionally, it could take some time, so don't hurry it.

Make sure you pay attention to any verbal or nonverbal signs that the other person may be using to guide you toward your desired outcome. When negotiating, it's important to pay attention, observe body language, comprehend the methods of the other side, and answer in a way that will be acceptable.

The key to completing this phase is to avoid arguing. Doing so could distract you from the main idea. Make sure you're prepared to make concessions if necessary. After all, there is some give and take when bargaining.

Closure

It's time to wrap up the discussions after everyone is satisfied with the outcome. The conclusion includes reaching a consensus and establishing it. This might take the shape of a written or verbal contract. The latter is often preferable since it explains each party's viewpoint in detail. Ensure that each partner is aware of the specifics and expectations. Include any compromises or repercussions that may result from one or more of you failing to uphold your half of the bargain.

Advice for Negotiation
Not everyone has the aptitude required for effective negotiation. However, there are a few things you can do to better advance your cause:

Defend Your Stand: Never enter discussions without having evidence to support your viewpoint. Bring material with you to demonstrate your homework and commitment to the offer.
Take a step into their shoes: Holding your ground has no negative consequences. Although you shouldn't exceed your budgetary constraints—for example, if you're purchasing a house or automobile, don't spend more money than you have to—remember that the other party has similar limits. There is nothing wrong with attempting to understand the other person's

viewpoint and the potential reasons why they may reject your offer.

Take Away the Emotion: It's simple to become involved and let your emotions influence you, particularly if you have a strong stake in the result. The best course of action is to control your emotions before you begin.

Recognize When to Stop: Knowing your breaking point before you start bargaining is a smart idea. If the negotiations remain stagnant, there is little use in attempting to convince the opposing side of your position.

Qualities of a Good Negotiator

Not everyone has an easy time negotiating. It is often referred to as an art because of this. Some individuals have innate talent, but others need to work on their abilities. Whatever end of the spectrum you fall on, there are several skills you need to have to be an effective negotiator. Some of them are:

Listening

Thinking quickly, succinctly, and logically

the capacity to perform well under duress
Putting your ideas into words
Ability to convince Flexibility
being knowledgeable and ready
When Talks Fall Through
Even the most skilled negotiators sometimes struggle to agree. After all, the procedure calls for some compromise. It's possible that one side is stubborn and doesn't want to compromise at all. Other problems that might prevent negotiations from moving forward include a lack of communication, a feeling of fear, or even a lack of trust between the parties. Frustration and, in certain situations, fury might result from these challenges. Parties may end up arguing with one another if the discussions go south.

The best (and sometimes the only) course of action for the parties in this situation is to leave. Eliminating yourself from the situation offers everyone time to collect their thoughts, and it could even help you both return to the negotiating table with a cool head.

How Come Negotiation Is So Vital?
Whether it is done for the interests of a person, a company, or the government, negotiation is crucial for a variety of reasons. It enables you to progress and go forward in life and/or your work. The ability to negotiate helps individuals in resolving disputes and generating value for themselves.

What Characterizes a Good Negotiator?
A competent negotiator has to have a variety of skills, such as the capacity to listen, think clearly under duress, be eloquent, and be prepared to compromise. It also helps if you have persuasive skills and are prepared with some background information on the other side.

How Can I Bargain My Salary?

Having a plan in place is the greatest approach to negotiating your compensation. Provide specific justifications for why you deserve a raise or a certain compensation. If you can support your request with data (sales statistics, months when you met or surpassed quotas or targets, and any customer or colleague testimonials), that would be helpful.

the conclusion
The skill of negotiating is crucial in the world of business. Additionally, it manifests itself in our daily life. Every day, parents and their children negotiate allowances, businesses and governments negotiate contracts, and businesses and governments negotiate trade agreements. Whatever you're negotiating, being a good negotiator involves listening, making concessions, and accepting the other side's perspective. However, arguing never solves anything. Therefore, being prepared for setbacks might help you achieve your final objective.

Chapter 2

Mastering the art of Negotiation

Many individuals think that there must be a winner and a loser in each negotiation because it is "all or nothing." Nothing is more false than it is. Although attaining what you want is undoubtedly the aim of negotiation, the finest agreements—the ones that endure—incorporate terms and suggestions from both sides.

Before any negotiations
A person should consider their goals for the negotiating process before engaging in any formal negotiations. Therefore, it makes sense to write down particular objectives or desired results. Be positive. What is your transaction would you consider a "home run"? The opposing side might just agree to all of your demands to resolve this. The next step is for them to come up with several

backup plans that they are confident in and would still close the transaction. The goal is to have considered as many different possibilities as you can. Finding (or attempting to find) any possible holes in the position of the opposition should be the next step. For instance, it is important knowledge that may be utilized in negotiations if one party in a real estate deal is aware that the other side must sell a certain property or risk experiencing a liquidity crisis. Finding your shortcomings is crucial. This is due to the possibility that a prepared side might utilize the other party's shortcomings to its advantage and win the negotiation. Help both sides more clearly define a possible region of middle ground, at the very least.

Another pre-negotiation practice is to create a list of benefits that their proposal would have for the other side. Most people don't do this, but they should. To advance the cause and/or find some common ground, it makes sense to bring up the major issues on this list during the actual negotiation with the counterparty.

Again using real estate as an example, one party (in this instance a firm) can claim that their offer for a certain property is more advantageous than others (even if it is lower in dollars) since it is an all-cash offer as opposed to riskier financing or a stock exchange. The chances of closing the transaction rise when the negotiator clearly articulates the benefits to both sides.

The Personal Negotiation

Each side should ideally state its aims and objectives from the beginning. This makes it possible for each negotiator to understand where the other is coming from. Additionally, it creates the framework for an interactive discussion. Each side may now provide its backup plans and counterproposals to reach an agreement.

However, in addition to the initial exchange of ideas, there are additional steps that negotiators may take to improve their prospects of winning the contract.

As an example, consider body language analysis.

Was your suggestion accepted? Direct eye contact and head nodding are indicative of success. Arms folded over the chest, reluctance to eye contact, or a slight head movement that seems to be a "no" are all examples of negative indications. The next time you pose a question, pay close attention. You'll see that a person's body language often reveals a great deal about their underlying emotions.

Via Phone
Body language cannot be read during a phone conversation during a negotiation. As a result, the negotiator must make every effort to listen to and understand his adversary. Long pauses often indicate hesitation or thought about the offer from

the other side. The opposite party may, however, be quite receptive to the proposition and just need a little prodding to clinch the deal if they make startling exclamations or respond abnormally quickly (in a friendly voice).

through mail or email
Email or postal correspondence used for negotiations (such as in residential real estate purchases) is a whole separate species.

Here is a few pieces of advice:

A party may indicate that they are open to a certain proposition by using ambiguous language or expressions. Look for words like "can," "perhaps," "maybe," "maybe," or "acceptable" in particular. Additionally, the use of expressions like "looking forward to it" or "anxiously anticipating your reply" may indicate that the party is excited and/or confident that a deal will be achieved soon.

See if you can combine any of the ideas included in the original or counter-proposal from the other party into your own, then quickly close the transaction. If reaching a compromise on a specific matter is not feasible, suggest additional options that you believe would be agreeable to both sides.

A more formal contract that reflects the agreements reached during the discussion is necessary, too. To that aim, shortly after the discussion process is over, have a lawyer prepare a formal contract, and make sure that everyone signs it on time.

Not Agreed? Not to Worry

Leave the door open for further discussion if an agreement cannot be achieved in one sitting or phone conversation. Schedule more meetings if you can. Don't worry; if you phrase your request correctly, it won't come out as unduly nervous. Instead, it will seem as if you think a deal can be reached and that you are prepared to put in the necessary effort to make that happen.

Try to mentally go over what happened at the first meeting in between discussions. Has the opposition made any flaws clear? Did they suggest that there could be other elements that affect the deal? The negotiator may get the upper hand on their opponent by thinking about these issues in advance of the next encounter.

In conclusion, not every negotiation results in a settlement that is acceptable to all parties. If an agreement cannot be reached, agree to part ways as friends whatever occurs. Burning bridges is never, ever a good idea. You can never be certain when you will need to cross those rivers again.

Chapter 3.

Win-Win Negotiation

Here are some suggestions for negotiating that can help you succeed.

1 Pay attention to the first 5 minutes.
According to research in the Journal of Applied Sciences, the result of a negotiation may be predicted within the first five minutes.

According to the research, to ensure that the negotiations go well for you, you should concentrate on "conversational involvement, the prosodic emphasis you should match the speaker's emotional state—and vocal mirroring."

The initial few minutes are crucial since this is when the other party is scrutinizing you the most closely. They are "sizing you up" to see whether you mean what you say or if you're just attempting to earn more money than you deserve.

In any case, be likable to avoid the other person shutting down on you. He will listen to your arguments throughout the negotiation if you can get his attention in the initial few minutes of the conversation. If not, your time is essentially being wasted.

2. Set your bar higher than you would consider acceptable.
In a study published in Current Directions in Psychological Science, experts advise that while negotiating, you should always start high. This beginning pricing will ultimately "create an anchor," having an impact on all subsequent numbers.

This indicates that you must begin strongly because it will induce the people involved to "choose the information that is consistent with the initial value and base valuations on it. As a result, in negotiations, a strong start often results in a strong finish."

Even if you are aware that the amount is absurdly more than what you would consider acceptable, no one else is aware of this. The other side can only speculate since they don't know.

3. You need to present your cases first.
According to this Harvard Business School research, you need to constantly think about going first in a negotiation. What are the advantages of making the first offer before listening to what the other side has to say?

All of this leads back to the "anchor" number we spoke about previously. If you are the first to go, you get to choose the anchor number, which will be used to compare or relate all subsequent numbers.

Making the initial offer will "anchor the discussion in your favor," the research claims.

Since it's quite uncommon for someone who lacks confidence and authority to ever make the initial offer, doing so will also demonstrate to the other party your confidence.

4. Demonstrate your enthusiasm.
If you're glad, smile to convey your satisfaction. Make it clear to the other person that you don't agree with what they are saying by expressing your feelings.

Researchers claim that "the social signal value of anger boosts the credibility of the complainant and so leads to greater compensation, but only when the complaint itself gives space for doubt" in a study that was published in the European Journal of Social Psychology.

These emotional cues will show the other party that you care about the subject of your disagreement, that you have researched the issue, and that you are aware of the figures you are fighting for.

5. Have a coffee.

Research that was published in the European Journal of Social Psychology found that the more coffee you take, the less likely you are to compromise during a disagreement.

According to the research, attitudes developed after consuming caffeine "resisted counter-persuasion and led to indirect attitude modification."

The converse of this is that you won't make many concessions throughout your negotiation, which will usually result in "more agreement" during the engagement.

6. Persuade the opposing side that time is limited.

More people will desire something if you give the impression that it will be gone after a particular period.

Researchers claim that "sold-out items generate a feeling of urgency for buyers; they believe that if one thing is gone, the next item might similarly sell out" in a ScienceDaily article.

This is due to the misconception that if a product is in high demand or has a limited-time deal, it must be excellent. Someone else will move if they don't do it now.

7. Give them as much information as you can.

Just give someone as much information as you can if you want to persuade them. Quantity is preferable to quality in this circumstance.

The opposite party will now be "open to persuasion" as a result. Giving them as much information as you can help them "resolve conflicted sentiments" they may have about what they're hearing.

The other person will likely be impacted by all of this information without even being aware of it.

8. Distinguish people from the issue

First, refrain from referring to your counterpart as your "opponent." Make sure to keep your attention on the current problem and attempt to disregard personality differences. Be mindful of three things to do this: perception, emotion, and communication.

By "putting yourself in their shoes," perception helps you find common ground or a workable compromise. Empathy at Work, one of our articles, may assist you in doing this. You could be persuaded that your stance is rational, fair, and "correct," but the other person will probably be as well.

Examine, admit, and ask yourself why you are feeling the way you are. For instance, may a negative negotiating experience from the past be influencing how you act now? To minimize misconceptions, ensure that your communication is exact and clear. Utilize active listening strategies, such as maintaining eye contact, paying close attention, and waiting for each individual to complete speaking before responding.

9. Put Your Interests Before Your Positions
People are seldom "difficult" merely to be difficult, and nearly always genuine disagreements are lurking underneath

opposing viewpoints. Each person's perspective on the matter may be impacted by a variety of elements, including their values, beliefs, position, obligations, and cultural background.

Try to maintain a polite tone and refrain from placing blame. They are more likely to be open to diverse points of view if everyone is aware that their interests have been taken into account.

Consider that your employer could be under pressure to cut expenses if you're bargaining with him to get greater resources for your team. If you look beyond your two roles, you could discover that you share a desire to boost team productivity, for example.

10. Employ objective standards
This goes beyond just "laying out the facts," since differing underlying needs, interests, perspectives, and objectives may lead individuals to interpret the information in

different ways or lead you to only choose the facts that are in line with your beliefs.

For instance, you can decide that rush a new product to market as soon as possible after debating its launch date with other departments in your firm. There's a chance that your viewpoint may harden and that you won't be as eager to listen.

Yes, there is some evidence in the marketing statistics to back up this viewpoint, but there are also signs that postponing the debut until later in the year to coincide with a national holiday might also benefit sales in the long run. Furthermore, it would allow your marketing department more time to plan a campaign.

Try to settle on a set of impartial standards that will serve as the foundation for your conversation. Legal requirements, market value, a mission statement, or contractual requirements are a few examples of metrics that might be used. The adoption of standards shows a commitment to achieving an understanding as well as common ideals.

To go back to our initial scenario, you and your manager may decide on a budget as the starting point for a conversation about more resources for your team and then go forward with the understanding that any modifications must be done within this budgetary constraint.

Knowing Your BATNA (Best Alternative To a Negotiated Agreement)
If you can't acquire all you desire, your preferred backup choice is your BATNA. This differs from a "bottom line," which is a predetermined stance that might restrict your alternatives and perhaps keep you from coming up with a fresh plan of action.

Instead, consider your options and decide which ones are most appealing if the negotiation does not produce the intended outcome. After evaluating these options, choose the most advantageous choice to pursue as your BATNA.

Referring back to our earlier example, the negotiation will fail if you make a "bottom line" demand for two more departmental staff members and your employer rejects it. However, you would be in a better position to succeed if you began with this request but set your BATNA to get a commitment to training and updated software.

12. Create options for both parties benefit
Each party will probably have a clearer idea of the interests of the other at this point, and a solution could be straightforward. You could even be about to concur. If not, keep an open mind and utilize the negotiating process to explore your possibilities. If not, there could be an entirely different role.

Let's go back to our earlier scenario and imagine that you and your employer both have an interest in higher productivity but that your business is unable to invest in new personnel or equipment. This might be seen as a chance to evaluate working procedures, educational possibilities, and low-cost methods of boosting productivity.

Negotiation: Win-Win vs Win-Loss

It may be okay to ask for a "larger slice of the pie" for oneself in a negotiation if you don't anticipate working with the other party again and don't need their continuous goodwill. Often referred to as "distributive bargaining," this "win-lose" strategy is used when negotiating the cost of products or services (for example, a house or a car).

Similar to this, when the stakes are high, it may be permissible to employ legal "gamesmanship" to your benefit, such as testing the boundaries of the law without going too far into brinksmanship. However, these strategies might have significant disadvantages if you want to have a positive working relationship with the individual you're negotiating with:

When one person "plays hardball," it disadvantages the other person. Later retaliation may result from this.
The losing party may choose to seem uncomfortable and disagreeable if they have to meet a requirement of the agreement.
During a negotiation, using trickery and manipulation may erode trust and harm collaboration.

Chapter 4

Strategies for a Win-Win Negotiation
Strategies for Win-Win Negotiations

1. The first win-win bargaining tactic is to provide many proposals at once

When you simply make one offer at a time, you won't learn too much if the other side declines it. Instead of thinking about what occurs when you simultaneously provide many offers, each of which is useful to you in equal measure. Ask the other side which offers she prefers if she rejects all of your proposals. Her choice for a certain offer ought to provide you a good indication of where to look for value-adding, win-win deals that will benefit both parties. Making various proposals at once not only reveals possible win-win actions but also demonstrates your amenable and adaptable character as well as your willingness to comprehend the other party's preferences and demands. So, the next time you're going to give anything, think of offering three things that are valued equally. Ask the other side which offers she prefers if she rejects all of your proposals. Her choice for a certain offer ought to provide you a good indication of where to look for value-adding, win-win deals that will benefit both parties. Making various proposals at once not only reveals possible win-win actions but also demonstrates your amenable and adaptable character as well as your willingness to comprehend the other party's preferences and demands. Therefore, Bazerman suggests that instead of making one offer the next time you are going to do so, make three equal-valued one

2. Second win-win bargaining tactic: Include a corresponding right

A traditional win-win tactic in negotiations is to ensure that one party may match any offer that the other side subsequently gets by adding a matching right in your contract. Consider yourself the landlord haggling with a potential renter. While the potential renter wants a promise to rent the flat for as long as she wishes, you want to have the option of selling the unit to someone else in the future. You might maintain your flexibility while offering the renter the chance to avoid the upheaval of a transfer by giving them the ability to match any legal third-party offer. Matching rights may increase the likelihood of a win-win agreement in this way

3. Try a contingent agreement as the third win-win negotiating tactic

Parties in negotiations often come to a deadlock due to divergent perspectives about the possibility of future occurrences. You could be certain that your company will complete a project on schedule and under budget, but the customer might think otherwise. A contingent agreement, which is a negotiated "if, then" guarantee designed to lessen risk over future uncertainty, provides a mechanism for parties to come to an understanding while still going ahead in such circumstances. Incentives for compliance or penalties for non-compliance are sometimes created via contingent obligations. For example, you can offer to pay specific fines if your project is submitted late or consent to drastically reduced rates if your budget is exceeded. To include a contingent agreement in your contract, start by having both parties create their hypothetical future possibilities. Next, agree on demands and expectations that seem acceptable for each situation. Finally, be sure that your contract reflects both the potential outcomes and the agreed-upon penalties and benefits. Your chances of being happy with the available solutions may be significantly increased by a contingent agreement, which can also aid in creating a win-win situation

4. Win-win bargaining tactic #4: Agree on damages in advance

Another strategy to promote a win-win agreement is to add liquidated damages provisions in your contract that specify how much will be paid if the contract is violated since contingent agreements cannot predict all future outcomes. Keep in mind that if one party later sues the other for breach of contract, the plaintiff (if she wins) won't get the same products or services that were lost, but rather monetary damages. Therefore, determining in advance the precise amount that will be paid for each late or missing delivery, for instance, may simplify any subsequent litigation or other forms of alternative dispute resolution. Additionally, discussing damages brings up a fresh topic, increasing the opportunity to provide value. In this way, increasing the number of topics in the mix raises the possibility of a successful discussion

5. Win-win bargaining tactic #5: Look for settlements after a settlement

Think about the moment you agree. Although you are generally pleased with the transaction, you believe you might have gotten more for your money. Conventional wisdom is that you should stop discussing the agreement with your adversary and move on to avoid jeopardizing the transaction. Asked the other party, on the other hand, whether he would be ready to look again at the agreement to see if it may be improved. Tell your adversary that if the amended agreement does not enhance both of your outcomes, you are both free to reject it. This kind of post-settlement agreement may result in additional sources of wealth that you may share. If you didn't already have a win-win arrangement, it may also aid in creating one. Your accomplishment in negotiating your original agreement could have created the trust required to look at the prospect of a partnership that is even stronger.8.s.e.n.c.y.t.s.e.t is even stronger.

Chapter 5.

Everything is Negotiable

Everything is a bargain.
This is something that we have all heard so often that we probably don't give it any thought anymore. Take a minute to give the adage, "everything is negotiable," some serious thought. Ist das so? Is everything a bargain? What does it signify for us, if it does?

When Is It Okay To Bargain?
The practice of haggling over things is accepted in certain cultures; market prices are seen as a starting point for discussions rather than final figures. One of the reasons American visitors have a reputation for being easy prey is because this is contrary to how people in our society believe. Even when the price is far more than what the seller would realistically accept, we tend to accept things at face value and pay the advertised amount.

Even those of us who regularly barter abroad seldom consider doing so at home. We seldom consider that we may be able to negotiate a better bargain since it isn't a part of our typical thinking that "everything is negotiable."

In many situations, negotiating a better bargain is quite simple—you only have to ask! Rarely will the cashier offer to lower the price for you if you have an item that has a snag or a box that has been opened and resealed as you approach the checkout desk. You may be amazed at how often you will get a discount if you bring up the problem and ask for one, however. Never forget that you cannot get what you do not request.

One situation where it may pay off to be inventive during a new employment negotiation is with terms. Try to acquire the hours you desire instead of merely negotiating your pay rate. Discuss flex time, vacation, parking, insurance, the kind of job you'll be doing, and even how and when you may anticipate increases or promotions. If you take the company's offer at its value, your position is probably going to be considerably worse.

The skill to bargain may be quite useful in the workplace. In your present position, try negotiating for a higher wage package. Request a promotion, a more accommodating work schedule, better insurance, or more important responsibilities.

If the only option is too much, you may typically negotiate a better price whether buying or renting. Don't spend more for a skylight if the only model available on the lot has one and you don't need or desire one. If you are renting equipment by the hour and you only need it for one and a half hours, haggle to only pay for the time you use it. Try negotiating for a cheaper monthly rental cost or have the application fee removed if you are renting a two-bedroom, two-bath apartment but aren't interested in using the second bathroom.

How Should You Bargain?
If you are kind and approachable, you will discover that you can bargain in many circumstances and get what you want just by requesting it. Simply make a polite request and watch what happens. You could get a discount, a better seat on the airline, or anything extra for free.

The approach is key; in many circumstances, a kind or humorous request is more likely to be well-received than a demand. It could also be useful if you can convince the other side of the advantages. Sometimes all it takes to persuade a vendor to comply with your request is the desire to make a sale and win over clients.

The Mentality of Negotiation

Try to develop the attitude that "anything is negotiable" during negotiations. Try to conceive of a price as the first offer in a negotiation rather than something that is fixed in stone. You must also strive to get over your fear of rejection and your unwillingness to disrupt the status quo.

Make it a practice to request a better offer whenever you get the chance. Although you won't always get your way, you'll be amazed by how often you do. The worst thing that may happen, keep in mind, is that they say no. However, even if they first reject, you might still be able to compromise! Adopt a negotiating attitude to start achieving more in life, and you may decide for yourself whether or not something is negotiable.